HOW TO ANNOY FRIENDS

AND MAKE REALLY BAD
IMPRESSIONS

A BOOK OF MY REALLY BAD

JOKES

Y.T. Alexander IV

Copyright © 2016 Y.T. Alexander IV

All rights reserved.

ISBN-13: 978-1541016545
ISBN-10: 1541016548

http://www.facebook.com/howtoannoyfriends

This is the only none-joke entry which is actually funny - my Microsoft Word crashed as soon as I began typing the first joke. That's when you know the universe doesn't want this to exist and you definitely have to put it out.

CONTENTS

1	Comics and Superhero Movies	9
2	Medical	11
3	Truly Tasteless	15
4	The Obvious	19
5	Really Bad	25
6	Author's Note	35

COMICS AND SUPERHERO MOVIES

I'm going to see Batman v Superman in a few days or as I like to call it - White Vinegar

*

Puberty to a girl: Tell me, do you bleed? You will.

*

If Nick Fury ever met Odin... they would literally see eye to eye.

*

I sometimes look up at the sky and question if the plane I'm seeing is either a bird or Superman

*

How does Jimmy Olsen passive-aggressively curse Clark? He tells him "Eff you C.K."

*

I stopped watching House because the skinny guy with a huge god complex, who walks with a cane because of a crippled leg, never turns into Thor

*

What do you call Chris Hemsworth swinging on a vine? Thorzan

MEDICAL

Do dentistry students go to toothorials?

*

If doctors are so smart, why can't they find a pulse sometimes?

*

What do you call teeth that grew at the same time?
Coinci-dental

*

What do you call teeth that had an unforeseen tragedy?
Acci-dental

*

And what happens to those teeth after the accident?
They dent-een

*

What do you call someone who specialises with stand-by doctors at a hospital?
An oncallogist

*

That awkward moment when the person 'in the house' who's choking is actually the doctor

*

Anyone heard about the dental hospital's renowned success?
They're starting to get plaque build-up

Never trust a dentist who was once a police officer when they want to do a cavity search

TRULY TASTELESS

If one gay kills another gay... is that a homocide?

*

Are blind people see-sick?

*

Why do guys get morning wood?
It's called slee..piness

*

I shall call my dick 'Love'... 'cause it's a crazy little thing

*

Yankee Doodle went to town, butt naked on a pony.
Stuck his finger up his butt and shouted, 'Oh, sodomy!'

*

When Scorpion has sex, do you think he yells at his partners where to... come?

*

If Christmas is anything like me, it'll come early

*

Pretty sure Black Friday sales 200 years ago were quite different

*

I hadn't heard about the time Helen Keller and Ray Charles went on a blind date. It was sad since Helen Keller didn't hear about it either

*

Gravity is the number one cause of death for suicide jumpers

Every communion, millions of Christians commit cannibalism

*

What do you call a dinosaur with a sex change? A trannysaurus

*

"Cocaine is for wimps who can't sniff canned-coke"

- Anonymous Addict

*

Where do paedophiles go to bid? eboy.com

*

So did Patrick Swayze's ghost make pottery with Demi Moore yet?

*

I just took a dick pic. But looking it over, it was a Richard pic

THE OBVIOUS

What's the opposite of a fire ant?
Antarctic

*

My name is Dirt; bitches and hoes dig me... literally

*

I met a prostitute from Denmark, and her name was Cookie... but I don't really enjoy Danish

*

If Apple doesn't support flash, how do their phones take out photos in low light situations?

*

If Harry Potter had his mother's eyes, then why did he wear glasses like his father?

*

There are two kinds of people in this world... people who 'YOLO', and Hindus

*

I can't go to the gym because I get sick every time. Especially the abs workout... I just couldn't stomach it

*

Poor snakes... they're deaf and don't even have hands for sign language

*

Want to put on weight fast? Then use insta-gram

The pasta I had last night was cheesier than this joke

*

I think soap is the best hair magnet there is

*

Anyone heard what happened to the guitarist on stage?
He hit the C4 note and exploded

*

I have this joke about pizza – nah, never mind – it's too cheesy

*

I went on a date with this girl and we ended up losing our eyes in a horrific accident... we're not seeing each other anymore

*

I had a girlfriend who listened to Iron Maiden... I tried giving it a go and ended up losing my head

*

Why was 3 afraid of 1? 'Cause in a blink, 1 8 2

*

I had a girlfriend named Banana... but we ended up splitting

*

I was friends with a guy name Soap... but we eventually slipped away

*

You know you're looking up some really bad shit on the internet when you're incognito browsing on your personal device

*

Was Usher himself at his wedding?

That awkward moment when a girl gets a boner

*

Haters gonna hate and masters gonna bate

*

You know what's dread? A Rasta man's hair

*

Any number divided by itself would give you 1. Except A... because A is a letter

*

You know what I just realised? The 'gh' in high is silent

*

Tidal waves are like an emerging sea... and perhaps an emergency

*

Anyone heard the joke about the bread? It was stale

*

My jokes may be stale like old bread, but that dough matter

*

You know who would love coal in their stockings for Christmas? Bob Cratchit

*

You know who would make good Christmas stockings? Bob Crochet

*

Scientists have turned back time... it's now emit

*

I wonder if anyone ever called the police whenever Sting acted up

Getting a job as a park ranger seems to be an easy walk in the park

*

Where did the Transformers go for vacation?

Botswana

*

Ghosts are very unsupportive assholes... no matter what I do, they keep booing me

REALLY BAD

People who are commitment-phobes have a hard time killing themselves

*

If you stretch your picture vertically, then you probably won't look fat in your dress

*

So a guy married his old school Nintendo. It was a WedNESday

*

I'm so lonely, even LinkedIn doesn't send me email anymore

*

Why change when you can remain naked

*

Girls, if your boyfriend is anything like me, then you must definitely be imaginary

*

You heard what the exhibitionist couple did for their wedding anniversary?
They renude their vows

*

Knock knock
Who's there?
Stiller
Stiller who?
Stiller better story than Twilight

Good things in life don't come for free…so drugs…aren't bad?

*

""Intentionally using the quotes of others without author attribution is plagiarism and contributes to illiteracy."
- Rain Bojangles"
- Me

*

Regular people: I've seen brighter days. Emo people: I've seen darker days. Me: You want me to go outside?

*

I should stop shouting in my head… I may go brain deaf

*

In space, no one can hear you Justin Beiber

*

I'm not crying. My eyes are just allergic to hurt feelings

*

I didn't choose the mugged life… the mugged life chose me

*

Don't want to brag, but whenever I bathe… I hang out with my wang out

*

If Stephen Hawking is British, why does he sound like a robot… just saying

*

Once you go Black Fridays, you never go back TGI Fridays

*

What is a landlord's scariest movie? Residents Evil

Looking for a highly experienced author to write my autobiography!

*

What if the human race... was actually a marathon?

*

Wow, your cooking is so bad it turned my taste buds into tastenemies

*

Becoming a lawyer is hard since I'm always approaching the bar every week!

*

If I fib saying I'm sleeping on my bed... am I really lying?

*

The one major sign of drug use is when you sound like Dr Seuss

*

That awkward moment when one octopus catches another octopus watching finger porn

*

It's insulting to know that people on the street would beg you for money just to buy drugs... and not even share with you

*

That moment when a Jehovah's Witness knocks on a door... and another one answers it

*

Why did the man put his pants into the payphone? Because it was three-quarters

WTF Niger, you is 1,270,000 km^2... you big

*

Team Edward or Team Jacob? Bitch please, Team Rocket!

*

A girl and I hit it off today... till I was done fixing her laptop

*

Would a Geodude die if it gets a paper cut?

*

Irony: when the first name of an atheist is Christian

*

"I will not be silenced!" - K
Knee, circa 896

*

Hey baby, are you being followed? Because I've been seeing people behind your back

*

If someone says the time is half 8... Is it really 4 o'clock?

*

I won't be doing any "That's What She Said" jokes anymore. It's just too hard for me...

*

Anyone ever read the book "Men are from Mars, Women wanna blow Mars outta the fucking sky"?

*

What did Ross say to his cup of coffee?
"I take thee Rachel..."

Can I safely say that $1 is exactly 100%?

*

Bras... boobie traps I could never get free (of)

*

Heard they're going to make a movie with a green ogre in space and they're calling it Star Shrek

*

I suppose the average slightly-giant-sized monster is mediogre

*

A crocodile tried to talk to me very aggressively... it was a snapchat

*

Whoa, why can't Keanu Reeves eat his soup?
'Cause there is no spoon

*

There should be a PRA (party rock anthem) button on my Winamp... 'cause e'eryday I'm shuffling

*

It's no coincidence that male enhancement emails end up in the 'Junk' mail

*

The rain is so clumsy, falling all the time

*

What do I do when I want to balance a ball on my nose?
Alaskan elephant seal

So a girl I'm dating is the ex of my ex's ex. It sounds kind of iffy but she's hot so it was an... exception
*BRRRRRRRAAAAAWWWWRWRRRMRMRMMRMRMMM!!!

*

How do you know when it's over?
She changed her Facebook status to "Getting stalked"

*

What did Tuesday say to Saturday?
WTF

*

"You smell like a hoe."
"And how does a hoe smell?"
"Like mud?"

*

I swiped right on Tinder for Destiny but apparently she swiped left for me. There goes my date

*

Apparently, my ideas are not energy efficient since incandescent bulbs are still popping up

*

Normally people say that it's raining cats and dogs... we gangstas like to say that it's raining pussy and bitches!

*

Belly button - nature's lint collector

*

My foot is like a computer processor right now... it hertz

Where do we put girls who lie about their bra sizes?
That's right... the library!

*

I'm trying to put together a toy train but I ran out of glue. But I'm willing to use lots of gum so: chew chew!

*

Where do the aliens who conduct anal probes come from?
Definitely not Uranus because that's where they're going to be!!!

*

Why is it you could never get anything in Finland?
Because everything's Finnish

*

If you want someone to pose with a neutral face, tell them to type 'lol' on their phone

*

Did anyone hear about the leg that wanted to bend? Me either, but it seemed like it kneeded it

*

So after one year of Hogwarts, Harry Potter didn't have to stay in the closet anymore right?

*

That moment when you realise that time is Irish

*

I tried cocaine in Jamaica a couple times, but I could never get the jerk chicken right... bombaclat

You know what's really sad...and somewhat funny - a homeless turtle

*

Hard truth: you inhale odourless farts... all the time

*

I'm currently using an anti-prostate cancer technique

*

So apparently, a woman at a supermarket found an appendage from a foot in a pack of mints. Now police are referring to it as the case of the tic tac toe

*

We all have doubts, regrets and herpes but we shouldn't let that get us down

*

When someone says sometimes that the pain you're experiencing is all in your head... does that mean you're really having a headache?

*

The animals on the farm all voted 'Aye' for better conditions on the farm... except for the horses

*

People always tell me that there's always more fish in the sea. You know what else is there? Gallons and gallons of whale sperm

I decided to take images of a specific herb - which has medicinal uses and can be used when cooking - and use it in a video to raise much more awareness for it. I end up warping the images sequentially so it transforms from one to the other in a very cool way. If you don't know what it is, it's morphing thyme.

Author's Note

Interesting, you're here. I didn't expect you to make it this far – I assumed you were going to return this for an immediate refund, and realised there was more to life than a way to aggressive-passively get rid of people in your life. But, my friend, you have achieved total enlightenment! Now, you can entertain everyone you know with the gibberish-jab of the great jokes you've committed to memory and watch them roll their heads off yakking away at your stupendous demeanour! Isn't it wonderful? Doesn't it feel great? Aren't you reading this in the voice of Ryan Reynolds? Perhaps I *am* Ryan Reynolds, born October 23rd 1950-something hoping to break into the book publishing scene because I need the money. Maybe. And don't leave me a one-star rating – the book is worth at least two.

~ Y.T. Alexander IV

Printed in Great Britain
by Amazon